11/13

DATE DUE

KIDS SAVE
THE EARTH

RECYCLE
Every Day

by Tammy Gagne

Amicus High Interest is published by Amicus
P.O. Box 1329, Mankato, MN 56002
www.amicuspublishing.us

Library of Congress Cataloging-in-Publication Data
Gagne, Tammy.
  Recycle every day / Tammy Gagne.
      pages cm. -- (Kids save the Earth)
  Includes bibliographical references and index.
  ISBN 978-1-60753-520-1 (hardcover) -- ISBN 978-1-60753-548-5 (eBook)
  1. Recycling (Waste, etc.)--Juvenile literature. I. Title.
  TD794.5.G34 2013
  363.72'82--dc23
                                        2013010609

Photo Credits: Michal Modzelewski/Shutterstock Images, cover;
Shutterstock Images, 2, 6, 11 (top right), 11 (bottom right), 20, 22; Steshkin
Yevgeniy/Shutterstock Images, 4; RT Images/Shutterstock Images, 9 (top
left), 9 (top right), 9 (bottom); Fernando Cortes/Shutterstock Images, 11
(top left); Evgeny Karandaev/Shutterstock Images, 11 (top center); Rob
Wilson/Shutterstock Images, 11 (bottom left); BMJ/Shutterstock Images,
13; Ivonne Wierink/Shutterstock Images, 14; Jaimie Duplass/Shutterstock
Images, 17; Zigzag Mountain Art/Shutterstock Images, 18

Produced for Amicus by The Peterson Publishing Company
and Red Line Editorial.

Editor Jenna Gleisner
Designer Becky Daum
Printed in the United States of America
Mankato, MN
July, 2013
PA 1938
10 9 8 7 6 5 4 3 2 1

TABLE OF CONTENTS

TOO MUCH TRASH

We make trash every day.
Where does it all go? Most of it
is burned. A lot of it is put in a
landfill.

How It Works

A landfill is a big hole in the ground.
Trash is dumped in. Then dirt gets
put on top.

RECYCLE

Trash is bad for the earth. We can make less of it. One way is **recycling.** Recycling helps keep trash out of landfills. There are many things we can recycle.

RECYCLE OLD FOR NEW

Cans, jars, bottles, and paper can all be recycled. Do not put them in the trash. Sort them in bins. These items can be made into new things. Old bottles can be made into new ones.

Glass

Paper

Plastic

HOW RECYCLING WORKS

A truck takes old **plastic** bottles to a recycling center. The bottles get cut into pieces. Then they are melted and turned into new plastic. Then it is used to make new things.

RECYCLE FOOD

You can even recycle food trash.

Save food you do not eat. Use it

to start a **compost** pile.

How It Works

The compost pile will break down.
Then you can add it to your plants.
It becomes food for your garden.
Plants use it to grow.

REUSE IT

Another way to make less trash is to reuse. This means using items more than one time. Pack your lunch in a **reusable** bag or box. You can use it again and again.

SAVE PAPER

Trees are cut down to make paper. You can reuse paper. Write on both sides. Reuse it if you only use half. This helps save trees.

Let's Do It

Reuse newspaper. Save the Sunday comics. Wrap a gift with them. This will save wrapping paper.

FUN WAYS TO RECYCLE

You can recycle and reuse many things. Save a jar. Make it into a bank. Or use it for small plants.

Let's Do It

Save a soup can. Make it into a pencil holder. You can draw on a piece of paper. Then glue the paper to the can.

OTHER PLACES TO RECYCLE

You can recycle and reuse many things. Carry items home from the store in a tote bag. Reuse it each time you shop. This will save paper or plastic bags. Where else can you recycle and reuse?

GET STARTED TODAY

- Collect bottles, cans, and paper to recycle.

- Use a tote bag at the store.

- Pack a reusable bag or box for lunch.

- Write on both sides of your paper.

- Make a glass bottle into a vase.

- Make a jar into a bank.

WORDS TO KNOW

compost – a mix of old foods put over soil to help plants grow

landfill – a place where garbage is dumped

plastic – a material that can be melted and made into different shapes

recycling – processing old items, such as glass, plastic, cans, and paper, so they can be used to make new items

reusable – able to be used again instead of being thrown in the trash

LEARN MORE

Books

Alter, Anna. *What Can You Do with an Old Red Shoe?* New York: Henry Holt, 2009.

Barnham, Kay. *Recycle.* New York: Crabtree Publishing, 2008.

Web Sites

EcoKids
http://www.ecokids.ca/pub/index.cfm
Play games, read stories, and learn facts about saving the earth.

National Geographic Kids
http://kids.nationalgeographic.com/kids/games/actiongames/recycle-roundup/
Play Recycle Roundup, and help Gus sort out trash and recyclable items.

US Environmental Protection Agency
http://www.epa.gov/recyclecity/mainmap.htm
Visit the different parts of Recycle City to learn more about recycling and waste.

INDEX